THE POWER OF THE INNER EYE

BERNARD H. HAMILTON

The Power Of The Inner Eye
Copyright © 2022 by Bernard H. Hamilton

All rights reserved. No part of this publication may be reproduced, distributed, or transmitted in any form or by any means, including photocopying, recording, or other electronic or mechanical methods, without the prior written permission of the author, except in the case of brief quotations embodied in critical reviews and certain other non-commercial uses permitted by copyright law.

ISBN
978-1-956529-64-7 (Paperback)
978-1-956529-63-0 (eBook)

Contents

Chapter 1 Law of Attraction Biblically Speaking 4

Chapter 2 The Power of the Transformed Mindset 17

Chapter 3 The Tug-of-War Within the Mind's Eye.............25

Chapter 4 Seeing What You Want to Materialize 36

Chapter 5 Gratitude in Your Daily Life 45

Chapter 6 Meditating for Inner Peace................................58

Chapter 7 The Kingdom of God Within...........................65

Chapter 8 From a Biblical Perspective – Take Action!........75

Preface

This book is written on the Law of Attract from a biblical perspective with the Power of the Inner Eye magnified in hopes of helping people live resiliently who have given up on their faith regarding this Universal Law in a way not taught or explained correctly in most religious settings. As a result, far too many people have given up on even trying to live a faith based life on reap/sow principles because of the shallowness of teachers not digging deep enough into the scriptures to fully unearth the powerful truths available to all humanity.

My goal is not to wow the reader with cold sterile theological orthodoxy. On the contrary, it is to present simple truth that even a young child can understand. Why do so many people give up on their dreams when setbacks occur in their lives? Why do men and women refuse to arise when disappointment arrives? Why do so many people say, "This stuff doesn't work?" It is because so many in this world continue to compare apples to oranges in relation to what they say as oppose to what they actual feel and do. I am here to encourage you to resist giving up on your dreams, your relationships, your career, the entrepreneurial pursuits, and yourself.

"But Bernard, I have been pleading with God all my life and nothing seems to work." What am I doing wrong?" "Why can't I get it right?" I am here to tell you that The Law of Attraction is real, from a biblical perspective. So, do not give up. You will learn how to truly be what you want to be, do what you want to do, and have what you want to have, IF you will apply the principles that I'm about to teach you correctly and biblically. It is deeper than what some of you have been taught incorrectly all your lives. And although some of you will find it hard to grasp some of the quantum physic "mind science," IF you will learn to resiliently apply the Law of Attraction "Reap/Sow" principles, you will see for yourself what many have learned about truly walking by faith without the assistance of physical sight.

With so many people in the world succumbing to fear, depression, and mediocracy, it's time for us to embrace a belief system that will inspire us to rise above the negative attitudes that keep us from reaching the top of our dreams and aspirations. It is time we live an abundant life, resiliently by walking by Faith based on Law of Attraction biblical principles! So, if you are down, it is time to get back up, the right way. Let's learn to align what we say with how we feel and how we act with The Law of Attraction from a biblical perspective.

As a graduate of a prominent Seminary in Dallas, Texas in 1988, with a Masters in Theology, majoring in Pastoral Studies, and Argosy University in 2006 with Master's Degree in Professional Counseling, I have always sought to understand life from a biblical yet practical perspective without being too preachy or theological. And the same is true with this book.

With over 20 years of pastoral experience both as Senior Pastor and Associate Pastor, what I will share with you is not new or original. However, the principles will be defended biblically yet practically in the context of learning to live a full existence here on earth no matter what outside forces try to disrupt your chain of thought and belief system. This book is for anyone, Christian or non-Christian, on a spiritual journey seeking to live the best life they can possibly live in spite of the detours along the way.

My intent of this book is not to lead you to Jesus, if you haven't already done so, but to how to truly live by faith with God in conjunction with the universe as the guide. It is to open your eyes as to how you can deliberately create an abundantly full life in the here and now knowing that the one true God of the Universe is still in charge to empower each of His earthly children to live through His unlimited power in pursuing their respective individual goals and dreams. So, I hope you enjoy the ride, on your way to springing back to the life you were intended to live using The Law of Attraction from a biblical perspective to manifest the good that you desire.

CHAPTER 1

LAW OF ATTRACTION BIBLICALLY SPEAKING

"Keep on asking, and you will receive what you ask for" (Matthew 7:7 TLB)

You are the creator of your life through what you can create from your imagination, but most people do not know that. Millions of religious folk are religiously blind to the clarity of the simple "Ask, Receive" principle of the Law of Attraction. It is simple and easy to understand. Yet, people have been listening to individuals who have no concept of how asking for what you want really works. They have this limiting belief notion that money is bad and that by wanting it is sinful, accept when it comes to tithing. In reality, money is neither good nor bad. It's merely a tool that we can use to help mankind from all walks of life.

Yet, you are expected to give money and more money to religious organizations, but you are not supposed to like having it to take care of your family or yourself. When, in fact, Jesus clearly teaches to "Ask" so you can receive.

Because of this unbiblical blindness taught in the religious world, we see people like Paul, first known as Saul, fight like the dickens to keep religious practices in place that serve no one other than the religious organization, at the expense of the followers. At one point, I was one of those misguided souls.

Paul was a religious man of the Pharisees in the Bible. He followed all the instructions and the traditions of his faith. But then, on the road to Damascus where he was going to persecute Christians, the Bible says that Paul "fell to the ground" (Acts 9:4 (NIV). He was blind for three days awaiting instructions from Jesus what to do next while in Damascus. And we are no different. Many are religious but blind at the same time.

Many of us are busy working jobs and living lives that we cannot stand because of the fear of moving outside of the familiar. And because we choose not to think outside of what we have been taught all of our lives, we labor to provide for our ourselves and our families. Yet, blinded to the abundant possibilities all around us to create our own possibilities and expectations.

Things happen in our lives that make us seem to lose our way; a misplaced dream, a devastating loss, a setback of disproportionate measure, behaviors and addictions that derail our journey on the yellow brick road, not knowing that all we have to do is change the way we think to the way we truly want to live.

You have got to understand that you are not in this world alone. God is with you every step of the way. James 4:2 reads, "you have not because you ask not" (KJ). For some, we feel our dysfunctional family, divorce, social status in life, financial demise, or lack thereof, limits us from moving forward into the brightest of possibilities, when you have the power all along to get you out of your current negative circumstances. We believed the lie that we would not amount to anything. Instead of following our own personal dreams, we followed the dreams of our parent, our family, our teachers, and even our religious leaders. Instead, what we needed was to listen to the divine voice within to do, be, and have what we really wanted out life. Because, when the scales fall off your eyes, your true mission for living begins, just like Paul, which leads us to the Law of Attraction from a biblical perspective. What voice are you listening to? Your own or the voices from you past that keep you chained to your past instead of your present moment.

Law of Attraction Biblically Introduced

The Bible clearly teaches that "with God, all things are possible" (Matthew 19:26b, NKJV), if you can believe it and see it in your imagination. And with The Law of Attraction, popularized by the movie, *The Secret,* in 2006, God takes center stage as the centerpiece in The Law of Attraction. However, the major problem though is that the biblical perspective is left out by a majority of the teachings of LOA causing biblical leaders to completely disregard The Law of Attraction as non-biblical or "new age," which makes no biblical sense at all since faith is based on the assurance of a future hope that manifests a concrete reality (Hebrew 11:1).

Jesus himself said, "Ask and it will be given to you; seek and you will find; knock and the door will be opened to you" (Matthew 7:7, NIV). This is Jesus speaking from a biblical perspective. Yet, religious people far and wide think that The Law of Attraction is not biblical?! It does not make sense when Scripture clearly teaches that "asking" for what you want from God is biblical.

The New Living Translation reads, "Keep on asking, and you will receive what you ask for. Keep on seeking, and you will find. Keep on knocking, the door will be opened to you" (Matthew 7:7, NLT). It doesn't mean that there won't be setbacks along the way, but you are to "keep pressing on" (Philippians 3:13).

It is so difficult for millions of religious people to see that God is ready and able to help you where you are through His presence and power that is already inside of you. What? God's power is inside of me?! If you can see it, you can receive it.

Jesus said, "You won't be able to say, 'Here it is!' or 'There!' for behold" (Luke 17:21, NLT), "the kingdom of God is within you" (Luke 17:21, KJV). Put another way, you do not have to look for the Kingdom of God outside you, on a mountain top, or in the heavenly places, or in your religious meeting place, because God's Kingdom resides within your heart and soul. And now it is up to you to learn how to use the awesome power that is within you, through your thoughts, imagination, your feelings, and your belief system, about God and about yourself. It is right there at your disposable if you can learn to practice the reap/sow principles tattooed all through the Scriptures known to a multitude as The Law of Attraction. These biblical principles, utilized the way they are intended to be used, will change your life supernaturally forever. It does not matter what your situation may be. When you understand the power of God within you, you can deliberately create a life that you never thought possible. Because at that moment, you will finally understand The Law of Attraction from a biblical perspective manifesting all around you as you create the life you desire from within. It's an inside job that you see with your inner eye.

My Story

I was raised the sixth child of six to Charles and Ann Hamilton in South Charleston, West Virginia. Dad worked hard as a manual laborer at the local chemical plant before being laid off from work when I was at the age of six. In the same year, Mom and Dad separated sending the kids to live with our grandmother on our mother's side of the family. This was my existence for the next four years watching my father struggle with alcoholism while my mother began a new chapter of her life with her new boyfriend whom she would eventually marry exposing all of her kids to the domestic violence between the two of them for the next sixteen years. We as children did not see this as odd on the West Side of Charleston, West Virginia as a number of our friends lived under the same circumstances. I didn't know about The Law of Attraction, although I was raised up in the church wondering if prayers were actually answered given the environment I was raised in.

My escape from home was through organized sports such as baseball, basketball, and boxing with additional time spent with friends in our neighborhood and beyond.

From an early age, my dream was to attend college so I could eventually graduate to find a good paying job with a company I could work for until I retired. Everything I would accomplish was based on human effort, alone. I didn't know God was always available for me to help me create an abundant life in supernatural ways. So I picked accounting as my major, not really having a passion for the profession, but to be able to live a decent life that would allow me to pay my bills, take care of myself and my family until I retired to collect my social security for the rest of my life. Yes, I know. What a boring life.

After graduating with my bachelor's degree in Accounting and Business Administration, I took a detour to graduate school studying another 4 years at Dallas Theological Seminary in Dallas, Texas with aspirations to pastor a church on the east coast of the United States all along thinking that my life would be financially secure with no real difficulties to concern myself with along the way. God would supply my every need in my quest to get married and raise a family. What I didn't prepare myself for was the financial challenges facing me as the head of the household. Also, I was dealing with limiting beliefs about money that stemmed from my early church upbringing suggesting that money was evil and "what will it profit a man if he gains the whole world but loses his soul" (Matthew 16:26,

NASB). These are limiting beliefs about money that mess up millions of people mentally worldwide regarding money. The Law of Attraction is based on what you see on the inside of you good or bad. You attract on the outside what you see and imagine on the inside. The power of the inner eye! As a result, you create your own external reality without ever knowing what you are doing based on your internal thoughts and feelings. What you think about most, you become. That is why The Law of Attraction can be such a powerful positive force in your life from a biblical perspective. This "Faith Power" is preached throughout the scriptures.

The Fog A Long the Way

Most people start out with good intentions to accomplish worthy goals in their lives before the challenges creep in. The allow their outside world to dictate their internal thought process. But then life happens; the kids arrive, the bills arrive in your mailbox or email each month at the same time forcing you to make tough decisions about which ones get paid and which ones won't. You move into survival mode instead of creation mode.

As I moved into my fifties, I lost track of my dreams feeling that I had accomplished enough in life to coast my way for the rest of my life, never thinking that I had the power to create the life I really wanted to create all along. And so, you go through the motions of life accomplishing goals that you have no passion for just to say you are keeping busy. And then one day, while I was watching television in my recliner, it hit me. I had lost my sense of purpose and was merely going through the motions of living without really living. I had gained 40 pounds doing nothing but sleeping my evenings away in my comfortable leather recliner. I was in a deep sleep walking through a fog not knowing where the light of day was. I felt like a former racehorse put out to pasture just waiting to die. And so it is with many men and women in the world. Most people never take the time to listen to that inner voice and think through their individual life dreams and goals because they do not think that the impossible is really possible, when in reality it is, when you understand the Law of Attraction and how it works in conjunction with the Law of Vibration. Vibration, energy, and frequency aligned create a powerful force. What you discover is that The Law of Attraction is the secondary law to The Law of Vibration. Vibration is related to your feelings and emotions, either positive or negation. If your feelings are negative you will attract negative frequencies from the universe, but with positive feelings you will attract positive frequencies. Either way, that is the law of the universe.

So, what happens is that millions of people go to work every day to jobs they do not like and live lives that they cannot stand. They no longer dream big dreams. They allow the negative feelings in their lives dictate their outer world. They just live with no aim or purpose as to what it is they really want to do with their lives. They become walking zombies more dead than alive not taking the time to think. They merely accept what other people tell them including the nightly new, the religious leader who sounds authoritarian, and charismatic individuals who sound like they have got their stuff together.

The reality of most people's current situation is that most individuals are capable of living an amazing life should they ever wake up out of their daily mundane routine of merely surviving. And it doesn't matter how old you are. You can be old. You can be young. But each person, should they decide, could bounce back to the dreams of their youth, simply by asking one question. "What do I want out of life?" That's it! If you ask that one question, you could possibly trigger a whole new beginning and direction for yourself leading to utter euphoria. You can begin to deliberately create that new life by writing down in your journal what you want believing that you can have it through the presence and power of God within you. Your whole life can change merely by changing the thoughts that you think. The good news concerning our human existence is that each one of us is resilient and strong enough to bounce back from any trouble, trial or tribulation should we ever decide to, but you have to change the way we think. You have to wake up from your spiritual coma by changing your thoughts. You cannot logically base your life on your external environment, or you will never wake up to the inner creations residing deep within your soul. The Reap/Sow Principle just like The Law of Attraction is based on thoughts becoming things that you sincerely believe internally while renewing your mind.

Why Some People Do Not Ever Wake Up

So, here's the problem. Paul writes, "So we fix our eyes not on what is seen, but on what is unseen, since what is seen is temporary" (2 Corinthians 4:18, NIV). Most people are focused on the external world instead of their inner world. As a result, many people have been traumatized by the events that have occurred in their lives causing paralysis of the heart and mind to think coherently through the thickets of their despair internally. When setbacks occur, they don't fight back to find possible solutions to situation. Instead, they wallow in a puddle of confusion not knowing nor trying to resiliently fight through adjustments that must be made to create their new realities. So, with the complete loss or absence of hope, millions of individuals give up on dreams and ideologies to settle merely to survive disillusioned by the harshness discovered in society as a whole. Does this sound like you?

Your heart has been ripped out of your chest due to devastations of varying kinds: You lost your dream job. The relationship you thought would last a lifetime unraveled before your vary eyes. A cherished loved one has died suddenly leaving a deep dark hole in your soul. Your money is low and all you can see is hopelessness, with no one willing or able to help you. And here in lies the problem. If you consistently look at your problems without working diligently to find your solutions, you'll end up settling for an existence that will leave you miserable. You will go through the motions in life accomplishing goals that you have no passion for just to keep you living in mediocrity.

You Are What You Think You Are

The Bible states, *"As a man thinks in his heart, so is he" (Proverbs 23:7, NIV)*. No matter what you say with your mouth, if within your heart, soul and mind you think you are nobody, you will create that reality in your life. That is the Law of Attraction. You attract into your life what you truly feel in your heart and soul. Because as the unknowing creator of life, your thoughts create the things in your life.

I was talking to an extremely charming woman one day who was trying to make it in sales. This lady was witty, articulate and fun to be around. I would say that she was "Miss Personality." But when I encouraged her to get in front of more potential clients with all of the personality she brings to the table, she cringed in discomfort, because, she did not see herself as interesting enough to attract important clients. So, she hid behind a computer screen hoping she could draw customers through email marketing and flyer mailers alone. She was what she thought she was. Does this sound like you? Do you know who you are?

You can become what you believe you can become if you can transform your mind from a fearful, doubtful mindset, to one filled with confidence and exuberance which anyone can do with change thoughts, determination and persistence. This thought process is the beginning of a transformed mind which can lead to a transformed life. It is at this fork in the road that you can wake up from your fog in life to become what you really want to be. But you have to see it.

With Every Setback There Can Be a Comeback

Understand that we were all created by God to withstand troubles and disappointments in this lifetime. We can bounce back from any traumatic situation if we choose to do so with God assisting us every step of the way. For many, the notion that life is to be filled with nothing but peace, joy and love is generally tackled with the rude awakening of various trials along the way. Jesus himself promised that, "In this world you will have trouble. But take heart. *I have overcome the world*" *(John 16:33, NLT).* In other words, trouble is a part of living in an imperfect world that we inherited at birth. Yet, adversity can never stop us from succeeding at what it is we desire to accomplish if we resiliently press forward at pursuing our dreams with the right mindset. With that in mind, each of us has the capabilities to succeed in the midst of difficulty because we each have the resilience to bounce back to something greater than ourselves with God's unlimited presence and power always at our disposal. Jesus said, *"I am with you always, even until the end of time" (Matt. 28:20 NKJV)*. So, with God on your side both in you and around you, you have the power to accomplish great and mighty things through the sheer power of faith in a powerful, invisible God far greater than yourself. And that is why you are fully capable of waking up from your self-imposed mental fog to accomplish something great on this side of glory. But, you have to be willing to think.

It Is Time to Wake Up

The Bible says in Exodus 1-2 that Moses spent 40 years in the wilderness after he murdered a man in Egypt and then fled for his life into the wilderness. Even though he had been raised in Egyptian royalty, he thought his life of leading other men and women was over. But then God reached out to him at the burning bush to go back to Egypt to free God's people from their bondage (see Exodus 1-3).

Moses tried to come up with every excuse in the book as to why he was not the right man to help free the Israelites from slavery. Yet, God finally persuaded him to go back to do what God had already equipped him to do. And the Lord has also gifted you with special gifts and abilities to do mighty things if only we would wake up from our comfort zones to do them.

So ask yourself the question, "What do I really want to accomplish with the rest of my life?" From this moment forward whatever the answer is, you must determine to pursue your life purpose knowing that with unwavering faith, God can and will open the doors for you to finally live the life you have always wanted to live without hesitation. You will finally be able to define your own definition of success. Because, you are the only one that can dream your dream, and do what it is you really want to do. It's time to wake up and start living your life the way you always planned to live. So, let's get started! Visualize your dream as if you already have it, seeing and feeling the good life that you desire.

Call to Action

1. Decide what you want now (Matt. 7:7). "Ask."
2. Buy a notebook and start journaling daily what you want.
3. Write down your dreams and goals and review them daily.
4. Match the emotional frequency of what you want as if you already have what you asked for. This is The Law of Vibration, the primarily law of The Law of Attraction.
5. Suspend your disbelief of your exterior reality. Your external reality is an illusion. Think positive thoughts instead of negative ones.
6. Believe what you asked.
7. See what you want in your inner man's eye to manifest in the outer man.
8. Feel what you want in your inner man to manifest in the outer man.
9. Praise God as if He has already given you what you want because He has.
10. Say to yourself, "It's mine." "It's on the way." "It's on the way."
11. The manifestation has already happened. The transmutation is on the way.

CHAPTER 2

THE POWER OF THE TRANSFORMED MINDSET

Do not be conformed to this world, but be transformed by the renewing of your mind (Romans 12:2, ESV)

Limiting beliefs stop most people from pursuing and reaching the dreams and goals they truly desire to strive for. It is because most people have conformed to this world due to being brainwashed into believing they cannot do what they desire to do. They have been told that they are too fat, or too skinny, or too ugly, or too pretty, or too old, or not smart enough, or did not graduate from the right school, or simply can't achieve their dreams due to the family they were born to. That is why your mind must be transformed and reprogrammed to believe that you can "Do all things through Him" (Philippians 4:13 NIV) and the subconscious mind, because you can. But as a result of the power within you, awesome things can be accomplished if you can grasp the supernatural reality of God and the Universe conspiring on your behalf to bless you in ways unimaginable. You have the power to change your outside world with inside thoughts and feelings. It is how you look at things. You have to keep going. You have to take action. You have to keep knocking at the door of possibility. That is when the magic happens.

The Football Mindset

A football player came out of college never reaching his full potential. After 5 years in the NFL, his team was contemplating trading him. But then something happened. In his sixth year, he played like an All-Pro player. He played with confidence inspiring teammates to raise their own personal level of play. When ask by the media what caused the phenomenal change in his play, his response was simple. "I changed my mindset and the way I was thinking on the field." He said, "I began to believe in myself and began seeing myself as a star football player in the NFL." Of course, this could be any number of football players or individuals making these statements. In this case, it was all about a transformed mind being able to do great things in the midst of adversity. The player's mind had been renewed by transforming the way he thought about himself through believing with unflinching confidence in his God-given talents to accomplish great things with the power of God to miraculously assist him every step of the way. His new thoughts became his new reality. The Bible says, *"As a man thinks in his heart, so is he" (Proverbs 23:7, NIV).*

What you think about yourself, you are. This is what you attract. If you think you're a winner, you're a winner. If you think you are a loser, you are a loser. Either way, you attract what you are. You are the sum total of what you think. So if you don't like the way you think, change it so that your mind is renewed with new positive thoughts that allow you to rise above your old ones and your old life, manifesting your new life. That's how minds are reprogrammed and lives are renewed. And it can happen to you. You cannot give up. Stay persistent. Stay focused on your dreams and your goals.

When you do, you can become what you think about most, if you decide to put the work in to make it happen. Your dominant thoughts create your reality even though obstacles arise during your mental and physical transformation. How you handle opposition determines your resolve to get better and better instead of getting worse and worse. That is where resilience of the heart, mind and soul come into play. You have to stand firm in the face of transformational adversity.

You Are Not in This World Alone

When you hear some successful people say, "Put God first in your life," they are speaking from their own personal experience. And here is why. Because, they have learned that it is not enough to believe merely in yourself and your own personal abilities. You have to believe in the presence and power of God within you, who controls everything in the universe, who can make things happen on your behalf. Many successful individuals have learned that the "great power" that they believe in is God Almighty and is the one who opens the doors of opportunity and makes the impossible possible, who manifests your thoughts and dreams into things and tangible blessings. As you move toward your dreams with a plan accompanied by massive action, successful people believe that God will align their thoughts and feelings in such a way that all the resources they need to fulfill their goals dreams will materialize in God's perfect time, as long as they don't give up and continue to consistently remain steadfast. Put another way, when you make an effort to put God first in your life through prayer, faith, visualization, and thanksgiving, you are still destined to do on earth what burns in our hearts and souls to do in spite of the oppositions in front of you. Just know that if you desire to do it, whatever "it" may be, God will still align the universe for you to do it, if you consistently spring back from the setbacks and disappointments that each of us will face on this journey leading to your lifelong destination. As long as we do not give up on what we desire to do in our hearts, we are consistently learning to be what we were ordained to be from the very beginning of time, with the presence and power of God within us from sun up to sun down. If you can see it internally, you can be it.

Solutions Are the Key to Resolving Problems

Whatever you decide you want to do in life, your first concern is never the "how" it's going to come together, it should always be the "where, what, and why." If your reason is strong enough to do what you want to do, you can manifest the good that you desire as you remain refocused on your dream. The "how" is the realm of the subconscious and the divine inner man in solving the problems that you will encounter.

So, as the dreams develop into a plan filled with a number of goals, issues will arise. It is at this stage of the journey that solutions will have to be found, and no matter what the trouble or obstacle may be, you have to begin to ask yourself, "What is the solution?" From there, you will need a small notebook to begin writing down possible solutions to the problems. You'll want to write down as many solutions as you can before prioritizing from best to least for the purpose of putting together an action plan to resolve difficulties standing in the way of manifesting your plan. You have to learn to believe in yourself and the voice within. In time, God will give you the answers to finally move forward in your journey to the next level of your mission, if you do not give up on your desired plans.

This is how the mind is transformed through the resiliency of persistence and problem solving through the supernatural help of God. Many successful people have shown unequivocally that it works by believing in the unlimited power of God through the transformation of the mind toward faith, if you keep just fighting for what you believe in.

Jesus said, "If you believe, you will receive whatever you ask for in prayer" (Matthew 21:22, NIV). He did not say you may receive. Jesus said, "you will receive whatever you ask." You have to repetitively and consciously speak to your subconscious mind, again and again and again, until within your subconscious mind and heart you truly do believe what you ask for. And when you do, the "thing" God has already given you in prayer can be receive into your reality within God's timing. This is why a renewed mind is so crucially essential at this stage of your faith leading to external things manifesting in your life.

The Blizzard of 1996 in Gaithersburg, Maryland

As the Senior Pastor of a fledging church-plant in Gaithersburg, Maryland, I with approximately 15 other people had mailed out church launch letters to over 300 people to attend our first service as a local assembly. To our surprise, the weatherman was calling for 15-17 inches of snow with blizzard like conditions on the way. To our disappointment, we had to cancel our very first service. However, we received phone calls from people who had braved the weather to attend. Nevertheless, we rescheduled the service for the very next Sunday with more snow on the way. Our small group met for a Wednesday prayer time not knowing if 4 or 400 people would show up for Sunday's initial service. To our surprise, well over 300 people were in attendance with a number of them making the decision to join our fledging congregation. That was well over 24 years ago with the church still fellowshipping in their new church facility in Gaithersburg, Maryland and still enjoying sweet communion one with another. Obstacles will arise, but God will work out the details even when you cannot see them clearly for yourself. There will be learnable missteps in the process of your plans coming to fruition, but as long as you can learn from them, and adjust as a result of them, you'll be amazed how God will allow them to be worked out and manifested.

From Asking To Transformational Thinking

So, once you know what you want for your life, by "Asking," you have to believe that you can have what you asked for with all your heart by thinking that you can do things with God's assistance. You must think that anything is possible with God helping you create the life you desire. But for most people, their minds must be renewed into knowing that they are not alone in accomplishing their dreams, by eliminated limiting beliefs and thoughts that can stop them from persistently pursuing their goals on a consistent basis. This is all biblically based on the reap/sow principles aligned with the Law of Attraction.

Call to Action

1. After asking and believing God has manifested the thing you asked for. You will receive it (manifest it) based on your unwavering faith which requires positive feelings of assurance. Feel like you have received it. Visualize that you have receive it. Say that you have

receive it. Rest assured that you received it.Positive Affirmations are necessary to help change the minds perspective on God's presence and power in a person's life. Feel your mind with positive affirmations on the daily basis, in the present tense. Tell yourself, "I am rich." "I am loved." "Abundance is my birthright." "God has made a way for me out of know way."

2. With the transformation of the mind, feelings within your inner being will also change for the better in helping you vibrate at a higher frequency of faith, love, and happiness. Decide who you really are now and write it down reviewing your dreams and goals daily.

CHAPTER 3

THE TUG-OF-WAR WITHIN THE MIND'S EYE

> *Be self-controlled and alert. Your enemy the devil prowls around like a roaring lion looking for someone to devour*
> *(1 Peter 5:8, NIV)*

There is a psychological and emotional warfare being waged between the conscious and subconscious mind in gaining control of who you really are and who you are truly meant to be. As the old mind tries to usurp authority over the new mind, a battle for dominance will ensue. The brutal reality of attracting health, happiness, love, success, prosperity, and abundance into your life is that the mind is a battle field between what you were taught from the time you were born and the time you decide to transform your mind to something more positive and miraculous. Yes, a renewed mind is filled with awesome possibilities knowing that the presence and power of God within can help create in your life amazing outcomes. It is not only learning to control your mind but also learning to control your feelings. Because, when you can reprogram your thinking to unlimited possibilities, then, your health, happiness, love, success and beyond, can manifest into your transmuted reality based on the feelings that are vibrating within. And that is a powerful thing to witness and experience! Feelings are crucial in the transformation of thought aligning with the "thing" being manifested by God.

However, understand that you are a rope in the middle of a tug of war between right and wrong, good and evil, faith, fear and doubt, poverty versus prosperity. And depending on how mentally and spiritually tough you are, that will determine how successful you can become on your journey, because, whatever you are transforming to, you have to feel it with unwavering faith. And, you have to feel good about yourself believing that you are who you say you are even if the new you awaits to manifest. This is called generating the feeling of having it now even before you physically received it.

What You Must Do to Succeed

The Law of Attraction is really a secondary law to The Law of Vibration. The Law of Vibration states that anything that exists in our universe, whether seen or unseen consists of pure energy or light which resonates and exists as a vibratory frequency or pattern. This means that you attract the frequency that you vibrate based on your feelings rather than mere thought. This means that feelings are incorporated in your faith. Belief is a vibratory experience that aligns itself with God's manifestation of what you ask for and what you want. For example, if your vibration matches the frequency of the rich, then God, in conjunction with the universe, will shift rich opportunities around you to attract that same rich energy in your life resulting in a transmuted manifestation of rich opportunities including money and success. The word transmuted means to "change in form, nature, or substance" (Oxford Dictionary). So, if you vibrate on a low frequency of poverty and lack, then you attract that same vibration into your life. And if by chance, you win a lot of money, but you vibrate, based on your feelings, on a frequency of lack and want, instead of prosperity and abundance, then, you are destined to lose the money over time that you just won, because your low poor frequency matches the frequency lack and poverty. That is the Law of Attraction from a biblical perspective. James writes,

"Let not that man think he should receive anything from the Lord being double minded in all of his ways" (James 1:7, KJV).

This means that in the process of renewing the mind, you have to consciously feed your subconscious positive affirmations that overtime will raise your vibration level of the one you truly desire for your life. So, until you are able to transform your mind into a well-trained positive thinking machine, it will be difficult for you to break through to accomplish the things you desire to do, if your feelings are not in line with what you're asking for. The reason being is that distractions are always present to keep you doing what you have always done to keep you stuck in the daily routines of your past life experiences. You wake up in the morning and prepare yourself for another day at work. But you think about what bills have to be paid, that relationship that's not working, those extra pounds that need to be lost, the job you cannot stand, the future that doesn't look that promising. And the list goes on.

The routine for most people is simple. They get up, use the bathroom, take a shower, get dressed, eat breakfast, and then, they are off to another day of the same ole work routine, Monday through Friday that they cannot stand. And for many, even when they get to work, they don't actually start working. A number of office workers will go down the hall for a cup of coffee while shooting the breeze with co-workers, before heading back to their desk. Of course, if they are smokers, they have to take a smoke break at the smoke station outside before settling in for an hour or two of work, before another break before their lunch break. This is the daily routine leading to 2 days of relaxation on Saturday and Sunday before another boring work week rolls around for the same weekly work routine. The routine becomes so ingrained in a person's mind that the dream that drove them in their youth has been replaced by complacency to pay the monthly bills, keep the kids on track with their weekly schedules, save enough money for the annual vacation, if possible, and figure out a way to save for the future. Now mind you, these are all noble undertakings, but without goals to keep you focused on what it is you want to accomplish in life, your desired journey is hijacked by the cares of your immediate existence leaving you completely sidetracked from what you believe your true purpose and mission for living truly is. So where do you go from here?

The Plan to Gain Self-Control of Your Mind and Your Feelings

Here's the plan: Since the conscious mind only accounts for 5% of total mind power, the subconscious mind, that accounts for 95%, has to be hacked with positive affirmations that overtime will change the way a person thinks about themself and about life. Because, if you've been told and taught by people who said you would not amount to anything, you have to change those thoughts deep within your subconsciousness, and that take time. So, you have to start consciously affirming to your subconscious daily that "I am happy." "I am successful." "I am a leader." "I am prosperous." "I am abundant." "I am a winner." "I am a magnet for money." "It is my right to be rich." "I deserve the very best that life has to offer." "I am wealthy.". . . until you internally believe it. And, you have to tell yourself these affirming words day in and day out until you are able to successfully change the way your subconscious mind thinks. But not only how your subconscious mind thinks, but how you feel. That is because feeling is crucial in the manifestation of things materializing in your life. You have to start feeling good about yourself as you begin emotionally vibrating at a higher level of positive consciousness. You have to start believing that life is meant to be abundant as Jesus said in John 10:10, "I am come that they might have life, and they might have it more abundantly" (KJV). You were never meant to not enjoy a full productive life that you desired to live. It is your birthright to live a prosperous life, no matter where you were raised, or how poor you were.

Romans 8:26 reads, "We do not know what we ought to pray for, but the Spirit Himself (Divine Presence) intercedes for us through wordless groans that cannot be uttered" (Romans 8:26 NLT). The reason being that the subconscious works more with what we feel rather than what we think. What we think is left up to the conscious mind while the feelings are the arena of our subconscious who meshes with the presence and power of God within. And what a powerful fellowship! That can lead to some supernatural manifestations if the emotions are positively elevated to levels of prosperity and abundance with dynamic intentions. That is why we can become co-creators with the presence and power of God within. What a union! That's where the creative magic begins.

You Possess Gifts and Talents to Be Utilized

However, you possess God-given abilities that you may not even know you possess that others would find extremely valuable if only you could find the time to discover them and use them to make a dynamic difference in the world. All your abilities are bundled up inside of you just waiting to be unleashed for the whole world to experience. But your subconscious mind must be convinced that you can do both your family responsibilities while at the same time pursue burning desire dreams and goals that excite you like nothing else can. The power of the subconscious mind in the conjunction with the presence and power of God in you, is a manifesting machine if harnessed correctly through your thoughts, feelings, and actions. Know that you are creators of your own life through the power and presence of God within you.

The Tug-of War Between Your Dreams and Your Survival

Make no mistake about it, no matter what your dream may be, you still have to survive. You still have to make money. You still have to pay the mortgage or rent. And the kids still have to grow up and live, at your expense. Nevertheless, there are 24 hours in a day, and with a few adjustments to your schedule, you can still pursue dreams with positive thoughts and feelings that can change your life even though you may not know how the two will eventually come together. The key is "don't quit." You have to keep moving forward taking massive action that can ultimately lead you to path of your dreams and new reality. The shift first takes place with your transformed thoughts.

You Do Not Have to Know How It Will All Come Together

The HOW is the domain of God in conjunction with the Universe. Most successful people do not start with a business plan. All they knew was that they had an idea that they felt could help a lot of people if developed over time. And the majority of these individuals start with nothing financially, in a garage somewhere. Many started with a high school education, or less, and an innovative idea. But, they were willing to learn what they needed to learn along the way. Because everything you need to know about whatever it is you want to pursue is learnable, if you don't give up. You just need to know what you want and then to ask for it believing that it is done.

Make Strides to Get Out of Your Comfort Zone

For millions of people, their comfort zone keeps them from utilizing all their God-given genius. Their daily grind of survival leaves them very little energy to do anything else beyond making a living from paycheck to paycheck, until a paradigm shift explodes in their brain stating, "enough is enough." "I deserve better than this!" "I am going to pursue my dreams." "Come hell or high water, I will figure out a way to live my dream, if it is the last thing on earth I do!" The intention of their future hopes and dreams finally hit them. They finally make the decision to follow their dreams to manifest the life they desire.

It's Not About the Destination. It's About the Journey

Let me explain this concept in detail. Here I was enjoying an "empty nester" lifestyle." The 5 kids were all grown and out of the house. My wife, Denise and I decided to ditch the 5 bedroom, 4 bath, 5,000 plus square foot house for a brand new newly constructed smaller home in the Plano, TX suburbs in a newly constructed community. There we were in our new home that God blessed us to be able to build, without kids demanding stuff. My man cave in the upstairs bonus room, complete with full bath and shower, granite counter tops and my own refrigerator to boot, not to mention the huge flat screen television with 2 electric reclining chairs to come home to. Man! My journey was over, right? By God's grace, I had been a part of not 1, not 2, but 3 successful church plants, with congregations still growing and still thriving. In my mind, my work was done, right? I had reached my destination. And for the first year in our new home, although, I went to church and worked diligently in our real estate business, I was content to stop pursuing dreams and goals, because in my mind my journey was over, right? Wrong! It ain't over until it's over. Because as long as there is life in your body, the journey is never over, no matter how old you may be. We are here for a purpose and it is never to merely sit and do nothing, even in retirement. If you reach a destination, you then prepare yourself for another dream filled with goals to catapult you on to your next journey. Just like in a really good cowboy western, once the good guy has completed his task, he hops on his horse and rides off into the sunset to begin yet again another journey somewhere else. The journey never ends, until it ends. And, so it is with you. Your journey is never ending on this side of heaven, until it ends. So, as long as there is breath in your body, we sojourn through life with a goal in mind for the good of all who come in contact with us.

Opposition along the Way

Will there be opposition and obstacles along the way? Yes. Will there be setbacks? Yes. But at no point in the journey are you intended to give up. You keep failing forward. "forgetting what's behind and straining toward what is ahead" (3:13 NIV). Every opposition is an opportunity for each of us to learn and grow along the way. At no point in history has a successful person not faced arduous trials in the pursuit of their dream. If it were easy, everybody would do it. But that is what makes it exciting; knowing that in spite of the challenges along the way, you can still triumph resiliently through the ebb and flow of the journey, if you don't give up to manifest the good that we desire through The Law of Attractive from a biblical perspective.

You Have a Choice

Either you can remain in survival mode going through the daily mundane tasks of living from day to day, or you can choose to incorporate your aspirations and dreams into the journey called life in the pursuit of those things you truly love and desire to accomplish, while at the same time, enjoying a vibrant and invigorating life. The choice is up to you to ask and pursue those things that you really want in life by faith implementing Law of Attraction principles.

Call to Action

1. Fail Forward. Don't give up. Keep straining forward.
2. The Reap/Sow Principle and Law of Attraction works if you work it.
3. Face the opposition head on, and make the adjustments where necessary.

4. Review your goals in your journal daily, and praise God for blessing you with the answered prayer that's on the way.
5. Consistently think about things you want instead of what you don't want.
6. Do your best to block out the negative thoughts trying to disrupt your mind.
7. Get full of the feeling of what you truly desire to manifest in your life be it money, a relationship, a job, or good health.

Chapter 4

Seeing What You Want to Materialize

Where there is no vision, the people perish (Proverbs 29:18, KJV)

There has to be a vision of what you want in order for it to manifest. When you wake up in the morning, see what you want internally. That's where the power lies. When you go to bed at night, imagine what you desire for your life. Know what you want to be, do, and have. See it in the inner theater of your mind and feel the feeling of having it now. See that home you want to live in and walk through the rooms of the house. Feel what it's like to drive the car of your chose. See your significant other taking you out to your favorite restaurant as you gaze into each other's eyes over that perfect dinner. See the avalanche of money in your bank account. See the vision for yourself as if you already have it now. Do not worry about the money. Just go there in the figment of your imagination with the elevated emotions of happiness, love, success, prosperity, abundance, and money, because with a vision anything is possible with the presence and power of God within you and around you.

It was Albert Einstein who said, "Logic will get you from A to B. Imagination will take you everywhere." "Imagination is more important than knowledge." "Imagination is the language of the soul." "Pay attention to your imagination and you will discover all you need to be fulfilled."

Imagination is vision that if practiced daily through the art of visualization can manifest into everything you want to do, be, and have. It is that powerful. And without it, you leave out the secret sauce of manifesting the things you ask of God and the universe.

If you can ask it, believe it, feel it, and see it, then you can manifest it in your present reality, in ways that only God and the universe can put together. Again, it is not your job to worry about the "how" of getting what you want. That is the domain of God in conjunction with the universe. Your main concern is in the "asking" "believing" and then "receiving" based on visualizing that inner picture within your inner man. Visualize the END RESULT, with FEELING. If you can visualize it in your head, you can hold in your hand and in your life.

If you need a vision board to see it, then put together a vision board with pictures of the new house, that new car, the money circulating in your bank account, that career, that sweet relationship, that weight loss. Whatever it takes for you to keep your vision firmly planted in your head daily, do it to manifest it.

The Power of Intention Within Your Vision|

If you have the vision of what you want, then once you have the intention with the elevated emotion of having what you want already, manifestation magic begins to unfold before your very eyes. But this means nothing if you don't make the decision to pursue that dream to fulfill that goal with that crystalized vision from within. Visualize daily feeling good about yourself and about the world around you. Know that you already have it. God already said "Yes," to your prayer. Believe that you already have it. It's on the way to being transmuted into your reality. And be thankful that you already have it. We'll touch on gratitude in the next chapter because gratitude is extremely helpful in helping you elevate positive feelings that lead to abundance and prosperity, but most people have questions about the presence and power of God within which can block your blessings in the manifestation process.

In the Beginning, We Were Connected

As I wrote in *The Gospel of Resilient Living*, according to the Bible, once upon a time, man was completely connected to God with no spot or wrinkle. With no doubt, man believed in God's universal power, without question.

The major religions of Christianity, Islam, and Judaism believe that there was a beginning to the heavens and the earth with a powerful God as the creator. And with that beginning, man was made in the image and the likeness of God to commune with his creator and to live in perfect peace on the earth in complete harmony with the One who made him and loved him. This was a man made without sin, jealousy, or corruption in his heart. Every day for mankind was a holiday. He didn't have to work. He didn't have to worry about making a living. He just had to enjoy himself while connecting with supreme deity who provided for man's every need.

To keep man a little busy, God is said to have given him the responsibility of naming the male and female animals of the world. And because of God's love and compassion, He eventually blessed man with his own partner, known as Eve. Life was wonderful for the man known as Adam and the woman known as Eve who fellowshipped with God consistently in perfect peace. But since mankind was born in the image of God, with the free-will to make his or her own decisions, when a sinful element from the serpent came into their presence convincing them to eat the forbidden fruit God had commanded them not to eat, they ate anyway introducing into their lives sinful depravity causing a spiritual disconnect between man and his

God. As a result of this blatant disobedience, all mankind would be infected with imperfections that could be corrupted by a spiritual dark element led by the chief fallen angel known as Satan. With that fallen element now embedded, man kinds mind, heart and soul began to doubt the love of God causing man to fall further out of fellowship with God as Satan and his demonic cohorts became a bigger negative influence on the human creatures God had created.

As time progressed, some people even questioned the very existence of God. They have chosen to believe that life ceases to exist after death. And so, doubt of God's universal power is consistently questioned by some while radically believed by others. As a result, most people struggle through life thinking that they have no help to accomplishing big dreams apart from their own human effort. When in reality, the presence and power of God is always available to assist us in creating the dreams we so desire. God is always there around us and inside of us to help us build our dreams. Now that is the true secret that most people do not understand.

The Choice Is Up to You

Either you believe that God exists and is willing to assist you along your life journey, or you don't. This has become a major hurdle for people in the area of faith. People say things like, "I don't want to bother God with my problems." "I guess I will figure it out by myself." Nevertheless, the Bible teaches that in fact God does exist. He is always present to help us manifest our dreams. His supernatural powers are always available for us to utilize as his earthly children formed is image and His likeness (Genesis 1:26). We're told to *"Ask and it will be given to you. Seek and you will find. Knock and the door will be opened to* you" (Matthew 7:7, NIV). We're also told "whatever you ask for in prayer, believe that you have received it, and it will be yours" (Mark 11:24, NIV). The whole idea of asking and believing is a choice that each individual person can make, if they so choose. So, the choice is yours to make or not make.

The power of asking and believing is the first step towards your spiritual breakthrough from a biblical perspective. However, doubt keeps a multitude of people from genuinely applying the power of faith in their personal lives, especially when trouble comes to town. Yet, it is paramount that faith with the presence of God in the inner man and God's power in conjunction with the universe can create what you want and desire conceiving and believing in your heart that with God all things are possible to receive, "whatever you ask for in prayer." With that kind of faith, manifestation magic will happen.

Nevertheless, no one will ever go through life without having to deal with trials and tribulations along the way of pursuing their dreams. It's not going to happen. So, the key to our journey is to focus on what we want and desire as oppose to what we don't want. There can be no room for fear and doubt when pursuing dreams and goals that only God can materialize in our lives in the first place. It is God's universal power that allows the impossible to become possible. The Bible says, *"with God, all things are possible," (Matthew 19:26, NKJV)*. So, it is God's power that can make a thought a supernatural reality. But, we as humans must believe that God is not only able but willing to manifest our impossible dreams into possible realities. It is a mindset of belief in God's unlimited power that has enabled a multitude of successful individuals to fulfill spectacular visions in this amazing world. So, no matter what your circumstances are or will become, as you forge ahead with your life, focus on the positive aspects of your journey instead of the negative ones. If you focus on the positive, you will attract the positive. And if you don't you will attract the opposite. You must have an attitude of "never give up and never give in" while working your process and your plan to make those dreams and goals manifest through The Law of Attraction from a biblical perspective.

The Story of Faith in Someone Greater Than Yourself

God has blessed me to be a part of 3 church plants over a 30 year span. Each one came together differently with different setbacks and comebacks. However, the initial launch services were all exciting to experience. Family, friends and potential members came to support us on the first service. Seats were filled. People were blessed. And, after the first services, the future for each new church appeared bright. But then reality set in.

Over the course of the next few Sundays, attendance dropped considerably. The money collected on Sundays was far below expectations. Some people came and went. But the one tangible thing that did not disappear was, "The Process" of growing a church of The Kingdom of God with determination and consistency. And so, we set annual goals in growing each respective church. Mission statements were implemented along with small groups that helped acclimate members to the body of believers within the congregation. Music ministries were developed to assist members in their worship experience. Christian Education ministries helped members in their spiritual education of living a spirit-filled life. Outreach ministries were formed to help others outside of the local church experience. And over a number of years working "The Process" in ministry, God began to increase the ministry with new members, financial growth, and new opportunities to grow. God blessed with the positive results and we in the body of believers continued to work "The Process" of ministering to people. Because, when you base your ministry on faith, you leave the results up to God while you consistently work and refine the process.

The approach is no different when it comes to any other business or project someone may desire to work with. Many people give up on their plans when they run into difficulties. They want positive results of what they are doing right away. When those results don't happen, they become discouraged and begin to second guess what they are trying to accomplish. They allow the setbacks to disappoint them to the point of quitting. But when that happens, some people lose their sense of direction. They don't know what to do next, because their major purpose for living, in their eyes, no longer exists. Many people in this category lose all sense of purpose finding no true reason to continue pursuing what they use to consider their calling in life, not realizing that from a biblical perspective that God is always there to help in our deepest hour of need. With that philosophy on life, we are never alone. People will say "The Law of Attraction doesn't work." "I'm just wasting my time." "This stuff is BS." Yet, if you would just stick to "The Process" of manifesting, in time, you will receive. Just know that God is always available to help us work through any problem and dilemma, if we are willing to believe it, see it, feel it, we will eventually receive it. Just know that God is here working with you and within you every step of the way as you visualize that life you want to live. Don't lose sight of your vision.

Because, with a vision you will flourish instead of perish. Just stick to the process from a biblical perspective.

Call to Action

1. Manifestation based on visualizing present and future blessings as if they already exist now is to be practiced daily, in the morning and before bed.
2. Feel the feeling of having already what you're visualizing.
3. Focus your attention on the present moment and your future visions as if they have already manifested now. Release the vision for God to manifest.
4. Focus your attention on what you want and why you want it. Let God in conjunction with the universe handle the "how."

Chapter 5

Gratitude in Your Daily Life

Do not be anxious about anything, but in every situation, by prayer and petition, with thanksgiving, present your requests to God (Philippians 4:6-7, NIV)

If you think negatively you will attractive negative results. Like attracts like. That's not just The Law of Attraction that is the reap/sow principle found in 2 Corinthians 9:5-7. According to research from Harvard Health Publishing, in positive psychology research, gratitude is strongly and consistently associated with greater happiness. Gratitude helps people feel more positive emotions, relish good experiences, improve their health, deal with adversity, and build strong relationships. People feel and express gratitude in multiple ways.

So, when things seem bad and dire in a person's life, gratitude helps in resolving worry and stress while raising positive levels of happiness and serenity in spite of the circumstances. "Lord, thank you for a beautiful life!" "Thank you for money in the bank." "Thank you for loving friends." And you say these kinds of gratifications even if it's not true.

Gratitude Scenario to Consider – Your bills are due and there is not enough money at the end of the month. What gratitude does is help you eliminate the anxiety through prayer and petition, with thanksgiving at the core of what you're asking and desiring from the God within you as you visualize and affirm what you're trusting God for at the present moment. And so, you thank and pray to God as if all your bills have already been paid, because you see them paid. You thank God for all the money flowing into your bank account, because you see the money flowing into your account. You thank God for your great health and happiness, because you already feel the great health and happiness in your life now.

Okay. I know what you're thinking, with laughter in your voice, "Bernard, how can I eliminate the anxiety in my life with all the lack and poverty that I am now facing?" Here is the answer. You act as if, there is no debt. You are not broke. The bill collectors are not calling your phone, because you are affirming every day that "I am a magnet for money." "I am rich." "I deserve the very best in life." "Money comes to me easily and frequently." "Money comes to me effortlessly and unexpectedly." You have to consciously hack your subconscious mind to ultimately become that rich, prosperous, and abundant brain that attracts things from your positive thoughts while giving thanks to God daily from sun up to sun down. You don't want to be anxious, because it will attract more anxiety.

You have to decide what you want and believe that you have it, believe that you deserve it, believe that it is possible for you while closing your eyes with thanksgiving visualizing that you already have it. Then say, in every situation without worry or anxiety, "Thank you most High God for blessing me with what I want and what I deserve at this time in my life." Once you've done that, release the prayer of gratitude to the presence and power of God within and without knowing that it will manifest in God's time, and then go on with your day or your night. God, the universe, and your subconscious will handle it from there. Again, the domain of your "how" is the domain of almighty God.

God Is Not the Universe

Let's get this straight. God is not the universe. When you hear someone say, "Thank you universe." They are not thanking God. They are thanking God's creation which happens to be the universe. He is the creator of the universe who constructed it in such a way that sheer energy makes up it's construct with all mankind connected within this universal energy field. And anyone who doesn't understand that truth, the Bible says is a fool. Psalm 14:1 reads, "The fool hath said in his heart, There is no God" (KJV). Now that's a fool, because the universe with all of it's complexities, quantum fields, and vibrational frequencies manifests what seem to be supernatural occurrences and things every second and hour within and without of time. Ask yourself, how can you explain talking on a cell phone to someone halfway around the world with no phone lines or physical connections? How can you explain watching television or face timing someone on your phone with nothing but thin air between you? How can you explain a GPS system that can direct you from one end of the country to the next? It is the power of universal frequencies and vibrations that we are all connected to whether we believe it or not. And that same universe, the Bible says God created.

"In the beginning God created the heavens and the earth" (Genesis 1:1 ESV). "From the creation of the world, God's invisible quantities, his eternal power and divine nature, have been clearly observed in what He made" (Romans 1:20). "God's power is unlimited "(Job 36: 22 CEV). And what He has done with his creation including the universe, the Bible says, "God saw all that he had made, and it was very good" (Genesis 1:31 NIV). That's why we've been encouraged to give thanks always and to "Delight ourselves in the Lord and He will give you the desires of your heart" (Psalm 37:4 NIV), because we have all been made in the likeness and the image of God (Genesis 1:26, KJV) to be able to co-create our lives through the presence and power of God within instead of without manifesting the life we each choose to live for ourselves, with thanksgiving in knowing that "Every good and perfect gift is from above, coming down from the Father of the heavenly lights, who does not change like shifting shadows" (1 Chronicles 16:11-12 ERV). Refer also to James 1:17-19, ERV.

Talk about gratitude and thanksgiving! Infinite source and infinite wisdom originates from God, the creator of the Universe, that enables each of us to live and to manifest the abundant life giving us the desires of our hearts. So "Delight yourself in the Lord," be happy, be joyful, be at peace with those things God freely gives to you, with gratitude and thanksgiving because when you do, manifestation magic pours down like rain from the universe granting you what you want and what you desire.

Manifestation Happened in Seminary Just Like That!

After working 7 years at United Parcel Service in Charleston, West Virginia, as an Accountant, I made the hard decision to leave my budding career to attend Dallas Theological Seminary in Dallas, Texas, in the fall of 1984, not knowing anyone in the state of Texas. No family or friends, I just packed up my Toyota Tercel and drove non-stop. I decided to walk off the Corporate Plantation into the world of spiritual possibilities.

Since I had cleaned out my United Parcel pension plan, I was comfortably set financially for close to a year. During that time, I didn't have a job or a backup plan for when my money would run out. You know, it's amazing how holy you can feel and act when there is money in the bank. I walked around campus acting "holy" when other students talked about their financial struggles as a Seminary student while trying to keep a roof over their heads. I would say things like, "I'll be praying for you." "God will make a way out of know way." "Just give it to Jesus and He'll make it right." I said the right things not believing that He would really provide for them. I said that, until it was my turn to financially struggle at the end of my first year at Dallas Theological Seminary.

I had finally run out of money with no job in sight. I missed my rent payment of $450 not knowing how it was going to get paid. The payment on my Toyota Tercel was also due for $210 with no cash available. I was nervous and anxious as to how I was going to get funds together to handle up on my financial obligations. But I remembered one passage of Scripture that reads, "My God shall supply all your need according to His riches in glory by Christ Jesus" (NKJV). So, I began to meditate on that passage of Scripture in the morning, in the afternoon, and at night. I was 2 weeks late on my rent when I finally receive my eviction notice to pay within a week or vacate the apartment I was leasing. My heart dropped out of my stomach with fear and trepidation knowing that I didn't know where the money was going to come from. I began to walk around all day on campus and in my apartment complex saying, "Everything is going to be alright." "Everything is going to be alright." "Everything is going to be alright." I said it so much that I began to truly see it in my mind, and believe it was going to be alright. I began journaling my experiences on a daily basis thanking God in the event of what he was going to do. Acting as if my rent and car payment had already been paid.

I felt good about myself and my situation even though I did not know how I was going to pay my bills. But, what seemed like a call out of the blue, my old church friend from Charleston, West Virginia who also had left Charleston to go to Bible College in another state, called me around 9 p.m. one night and said, "Hey man, I don't know why you are weighing heavy on my heart, but I just received a nice size tax refund check from the IRS and I felt led to mail you a check for $500." I fell on the floor with hands stretched out looking up at the ceiling, yelling at the top of my lungs, "Yes!" "Yes!" Yes!" It happened just like that. I received the check 2 days later and was able to pay my rent with $50 to spare.

Okay, but what about my car payment? Being that I use to do janitorial work while in high school at a local bank in Charleston, West Virginia, I knew the ins and out of cleaning a building. So, 2 days after I received the $500, I received a phone call from a fellow seminarian who said, "Hey Bernard, didn't you tell me you use to do janitorial work when you were in high school?" "Well I have a friend who owns a janitorial business and he needs someone to clean out this newly purchased building from one of his clients." "He is offering to pay $250 for 2 days of work on Saturday and Sunday." "Are you interested?" Whoa! It happened just like that! By God's grace, I had manifested $800 within a 5 day span and was able to pay my bills in a timely fashion!

But what about having no job? No problem. One week after cleaning the office building just one block from the seminary, I'm on campus at DTS in the student lounge and a silver haired gentlemen walked through to buy a soft drink out of the vending machine at the same time I was purchasing one. I asked him, "So what year are you in," thinking he was a student.

He chuckled and said, "I wish I would have gone to DTS, but I'm on the board of the school." With a smile on this face, he reached out his right hand to shake mine and said, "Nice to meet you. I'm Norm Miller." Norm Miller happened to be the President and CEO of Interstate Battery in Dallas, Texas.

He asked me what I did before I came to Dallas, and I told him that I was an Accountant for United Parcel Service for a number of years. His response, "We're looking for a staff accountant at my company." "If you're interested, setup an appointment with my partner and let's see if we can put you to work." It happened just like that! And for the next 3 years, I was Norman Millers personal in-house accountant dealing with his personal and non-profit financial reporting activities. It happened just like that!

This was the beginning of my early understanding of praising God and manifesting from a biblical perspective in the midst of a storm, because I had to. Even though I felt anxious, I tried to focus on all the goodness in my life. I spoke positive affirmations into my life even when things external didn't seem right. And through remaining grateful for what I had, I discovered that abundance and prosperity flowed into my life when I least expected. Law of Attraction attracted money and a new job when I needed it.

The Greatest Resource Is Not Money

And yes, you can manifest money with The Law of Attraction. Yes, you can manifest relationships. Yes, you can manifest good health. But, the greatest resource at your disposal is not money, people, places, or things. It is the resourcefulness of people implementing a plan without giving up on the process and believing it will get done. If you take a look at some of the greatest business people on the planet, many of them started with nothing and ended up with some of the greatest companies the world has ever known. Their secret wasn't that they had a lot of money. It was that they were resourceful in thinking through the many obstacles to come up with innovative ideas that enabled them to amass great success in spite of their detours leading to their destinations. They saw it internally first before it manifested externally.

If it were all about money, consider all the former professional multimillion dollar athletes who made millions and millions of dollars who are now broker than broke. Sheer talent and skills do not always guarantee that you'll be able to keep the money that you amass. The question that you have to ask yourself is this. Do you have the wisdom and the resourcefulness to resiliently accomplish the dreams and goals that you want to pursue using The Law of Attraction from a biblical perspective? Because you can start with nothing and end up with whatever success you are aiming for, if you can believe you already have it in your imagination; not later but now. It all depends on how resourceful you are being thankful where you are while praising God in the event of what He is going to do to manifest your vision.

Church Plant from Nothing to Something with Gratitude

After graduating from Dallas Theological Seminary, my goal was to help plant a church in the Maryland/DC area with 2 of my seminary classmates. For weeks, we planned and prayed about starting a church ministry even though we did not know how many people would ultimately show up to attend the church services. Since my colleague, Bernard Fuller also taught at the local Bible College, it was decided that this new church would hold its worship services in the Bible College's chapel.

To our amazement, approximately 400 people attended the first initial church service and over the next 5 years the church continued to grow. After the fifth year, I chose to start another church about 40 miles away closer to where I had purchased a home in Gaithersburg, Maryland. But from those humble beginnings, now, Dr. Bernard Fuller not only continued to grow that initial church, but they were able to eventually purchase the Bible College property and the overall campus in establishing New Song Bible Fellowship Church in the community for the whole city to see and experience.

The vision and resourcefulness of the church leader, Dr. Bernard Fuller, and the people who supported him through prayer, preparation, perspiration, and financial support led to the manifestation of a great ministry still impacting the city for Christ. More power to them!

Just know that there is no trouble or setback too great when faced with resourcefulness of mind. All you have to do is pray for wisdom to come up with the resourceful innovative wisdom and ideas to resiliently push forward toward your ultimate goals, while giving thanks God every step of the way believing that He will do what He says He'll do, as if He had already done it. Know that God and the God in you can manifest your desires in supernatural ways.

Write It Down on Paper in Your Gratitude Journal

When you are working through problems where resources are non-existent, write down the possibilities that can lead you to the solutions you are looking for. Write out your perfect day, every day, keeping it fresh in your mind. It can be any number of possibilities that you write down knowing that none are impossible to accomplish with God as your power source. As stated earlier in the book, *"nothing will be impossible with God" (Luke 1:37, NASB)*. So, write your possibilities down and see how they will eventually manifest as you diligently and persistently work them into your action plans. Be sure to always start your day with gratitude and end your day on the same note.

Acknowledge the Power of God in All Creation with Gratitude

If it is meant for you to create your dreams into reality, you have to come to the realization that there is a power greater than yourself attracting all the money, the people, the interest, and the opportunities making your dreams happen. For me, that power is Almighty God, the creator of the universe who aligns the resources needed to make the impossible possible by thinking, seeing, feeling, believing, with thanksgiving.

The Reap/Sow Principle Mirroring Law of Attraction

Biblical minded people adhere to the reap/sow principle of Galatians 6:7 that reads, *Be not deceived; God is not mocked: for whatsoever a man sows, that shall he also reap*. This principle is the same principle many people know as The Law of Attraction. And even though some religious people may take issue with this analogy, whatever you think and feel, that will you also attract. This is the cause and effect passage that states that you will get out of life what you put into life. Your words, thoughts and deeds will cause an effect that will produce the life that dominates most of your thinking and your actions. So, if during the course of your life, you say you want to be a successful entrepreneur but most of your thoughts and actions are centered around spending money to entertain yourself with no thought of resourcefully planning to actually be an entrepreneur, then there is no way that you can be the person you say you want to be. You will reap in your life what you sow into your life. You will attract what you think. This is The Law of Attraction from a biblical perspective.

So, whatever you sow in your heart, soul, and mind, you can reap it in your everyday reality, with thanksgiving. As a mind thinks, that's what you attract. That is why the resourcefulness of your mind in the area of wisdom is far more precious than money because without the wisdom coupled with gratitude, the abundance and prosperity will slip through your fingers like water rolling off of a ducks back.

Intensity of Purpose Is Crucial to Gratified Wisdom

In order for you to be able to stay focused on what it is you want to accomplish, you must pursue your dreams with intensity of purpose. Whatever you want, you have to ask yourself, "Why? You have to have a big enough reason to go after your dreams with desire and passion, because with that flame inside of you, you will have the resilience and resourcefulness to keep on keeping on. You'll be able to weather the storm while waiting on the innovative ideas to flood your mind with penetrating confidence and assurance. With that purpose and passion, you will be able to harness the energy and thought provoking power that will provide you with the resourceful wisdom that is more precious than rubies and money. So, continually fuel your purpose and passion from within so that God will continue to bless you with the resourceful wisdom to make the impossible happen, as you consistent give thanks for what you have and what you have on the way.

Call to Action

Gratitude Affirmations to Quote First Thing in the Morning and Right Before Bed.

1. I am grateful for my health.
2. I am grateful for my happiness.
3. I am grateful for the love in my life.
4. I am grateful for my success.
5. I am grateful for my prosperity.
6. I am grateful for my abundance.
7. I am grateful for all the money flowing into my bank account.
8. I am so happy and grateful the 10 pounds that I have lost.
9. I am so happy and grateful now that I am financially secure.
10. I am so happy and grateful for my significant other.

Note: Add to the list where you see fit to be grateful, and by all means, be grateful daily knowing that abundance flows out of your gratitude. So be grateful always and watch your abundance increase. Feel free to discuss.

Chapter 6

Meditating for Inner Peace

> *After He had dismissed them, He went up on a mountain by Himself to pray. Later that night, He was there alone,*
> *(Matthew 14:23, NIV)*

What many wealthy people have in common is meditation. Meditation is their morning routine that many do in the quietness of their own solitary place, wherever that might be to open up their Chakras, but the chakra thing another is book for another time. They do it to clear their thoughts of all the noise of the world so they can think and visualize and re-energize their minds and overall bodies for yet another day of creation and productivity.

Breathing in and breathing out, focusing on the present moment with elevated emotions of peace, love, harmony, and joy while blocking out the noise of the daily grind. This is what many believe Jesus did as often as he could when he went alone on a mountain to pray and collect his thought while communing with The Most High God. And so, it can be with you.

According to the Mayo Clinic, in a February, 2015 article, "meditation can wipe away the day's stress, bringing with it inner peace." The article further states that "If stress has you anxious, tense and worried, consider trying meditation. Spending even a few minutes in meditation can restore your calm and inner peace." What you will discover with meditation is that it can give you a sense of calm, peace and balance that can benefit both your emotional well-being and your overall health.

Neuroscientist who study the brain have concluded that a brain detached from the past while focused on the present moment, mindful of future realities imagined in the here and now, is a brain filled with elevated emotions of peace and serenity. That is where neuroscientist would like for us to reside primarily.

Through meditation research shows various brain waves can move from Alpha waves which is frequency bridge between our conscious thinking to Beta waves which are dominate during our waking state of consciousness when attention is directed towards cognitive tasks and the outside world, to Theta waves which occur often during sleep and are dominate during deep meditation effecting our subconscious mind in a very positive way. It is at the Theta wave level that the magic happens when it come to The Law of Attraction and Reap/Sow Principle. So from a biblical perspective, when the brain is calm meditating on God's blessings both in the present moment and with conviction of "things hoped for," powerful divine things from the energized universe can happen in ways not comprehended by the rational mind.

What is Faith?

In Hebrew 11:1, "Faith is the assurance of things hoped for, the conviction (or evidence) of things not seen" (ESV).

It's like you know that you know that you know. There is a hope in you so strong in your present moment already receiving that future blessing in the here and now with feelings of assurance and conviction. In that person's mind, that "thing not seen" is already here, without question. This comes back to prayer, "whatever you ask in prayer, believe that you have received it (already), and it will be yours" (Mark 11:24 ESV). It does not say, "it may be yours." It says, "it will be yours." Faith is believing you are already got it before you physically received it. Based on your brain wave emotional vibration, when you feel it and you believe you can already see it, the subconscious mind in conjunction with God and the universe manifest the supernatural in your life, but only if you have the faith to believe it to receive it. It's when your thoughts, your energy, and your emotional vibration align at the same frequency to manifest long enough to transmute your material blessing. Yes, faith includes positive feeling in the process of receiving.

Romans 4:17b reads, "God who gives life to the dead, and calleth the things that are not, as though they were" (ASV). God has the ability to turn nothing into something. He can turn thoughts and feelings into things. As a result, we can manifest anything into reality, if we can align our thoughts, our visions (inner eye), and our emotions into what we believe God for, based on a faith of assurance and conviction. The possibilities of your faith with the presence and power of God within you, are endless. If you can learn to be a creator with your faith instead of a victim, The Law of Attraction based on the Law of Vibration will change your life for the better, no matter what your current situation may be.

God's Plan For You

The Bible says, Jeremiah 29:11, "For I know the plans I have for you," declares the Lord, "plans to prosper you and not to harm you, plans to give you hope and a future" (NIV).

The great thing about meditation is that it can allow a person to break the shackles of limiting beliefs concerning abundance and prosperity based on the incorrect teachings they received about money when they were younger. Money is not bad. It is a valuable tool that we can use to improve our lives and the lives of others. Therefore, money is good. I love money and money love me. I am not mastered by money. It is an awesome tool that allows a person to express themselves in very positive ways. And when it come to the plan of God, it was never his intent for his creation to not prosper and be happy. So, when you can see yourself as deserving of good things in life that prosper you and offer you hope and a future, that is an awesome vision to meditate on as you calm your heart, soul, and mind on a daily basis.

God's plan is to prosper you. Meditate on that. God's plan is to give you hope and a future. Meditate on that. Because, when you do, you will begin to attract success, abundance, peace, joy, prosperity, good will, and so much more into your life. Meditate on that.

Why Thinking on What You Don't Want Keeps You in Lack

Always remember that you attract what you think about. So, if you're thinking about not having money and worrying about losing your home, your car, your partner, your business and your health on a daily basis, you will attract what you don't want in your life. You cannot consistently think about being broke, or being sick, or being poor, and think that God and the universe is going to attract wealth and abundance to your life. Even if you win the lotto and you now have $15 million dollars in your bank account, with an attitude of lack and poverty as your mindset, there is no way you can keep the money that you've won. Consider the fact that the National Endowment for Financial Education (NEFE) states that 70 percent of lottery winners end up bankrupt in a just a few years after receiving a large financial windfall. Thoughts of lack attract poverty. That's why the money of a lottery winner who thinks like a poor person will eventually leave their bank account over time so that they can get back to the lack and poverty mindset that is embossed on their mind and soul. If you don't see money as your friend and your ever-present companion, money will flee from you. And it goes back to Proverbs 23:7, "For as a he thinks in his heart, so is he" (NKJV). This means that no matter what comes out of your mouth or what you say, the real emotional vibrations flowing out of your heart and subconscious are what you'll manifest in your life. Your thoughts cannot contradict what you say you emotionally believe if expect to receive what you ask for.

The Bible says, "Do not be deceived: God is not to be mocked. Whatsoever a man soweth, that shall he also reap" (KJV). This is The Law of Attraction on steroids. If you think it, feel it, and believe it, you will attract it into your life, even if you are trying to convince everybody else something different. God will not be mocked by your lies. James writes, "For let not that man think that he shall receive anything from the Lord. Being double-minded and unstable in all his ways" (James 1:7-8, NASB). And as a result, what God has already prepared for you, He won't give it to you until you are able to genuinely believe what you say you believe about your blessing that He already said yes to. If you think in your heart a certain way about certain things, it is those things that you will attract into your life. You want to be wealthy? Then, you have to think like a wealthy person instead of a poor one. That is the Universal Law also known at The Reap/Sow Principle from a biblical perspective. That is why meditation is crucial in the process of transforming your mind to one of faith, hope, and love. You have to clear out that negative energy in the inner recesses of your heart, soul, and mind. You have to believe that faith is not always logical in comparison to the illusion of your external reality. You have to create your own reality from within.

Faith is about thought, vision, positive feelings of a future hope, and the belief that God in conjunction with His universe, will manifest your inner dreams into your new external reality, no matter where you start from on your journey.

Call to Action

1. Make it your daily morning routine to meditate on positive things to calm your mind and clear out the negative energy in your soul.
2. Learn to focus on breathing in and breathing out eliminating daily thoughts and issues from the equation.
3. Meditate laying down and sitting in a comfortable position in a quiet part of your home, car, or while walking alone in place you feel at peace.
4. Meditate on what your "perfect day" looks like. What does it feel like? Where are you? What are you doing?
5. Find some good "Theta" Wave music on YouTube to calm your nerves.
6. Meditate on all that you are thankful for.
7. Meditate to release the stress from you mind and your soul.

CHAPTER 7

THE KINGDOM OF GOD WITHIN

Bernard H. Hamilton

"The Kingdom of God is within you" (Luke 17:21, KJV)

Dr. Steven McSwain quoted that, "it takes no effort... no struggle whatsoever to know and live inside the kingdom of God's Presence. Just a heightened inner awareness of this state of Divine Grace" through the inner eye.

Here's the problem. Millions upon millions of religious people consistently pray to a God or Infinite Source in the "great by and by" somewhere over yonder. They don't see themselves physically or spiritually connected to the presence and power of God from within. "The Kingdom of God is within you" (Luke 17:21, KJV). They don't see themselves as co-creators of their lives with God even though The Law of Attraction and Scripture clearly states, "Do you not know that you yourselves are God's temple and that God's Spirit dwells in your midst"(1 Corinthians 3:16, NIV). The New Living Translation put's it this way: "Don't you realize that all of you together are the temple of God and that the Spirit of God lives in you?" Everything you need to succeed in business, relationships, health, wealth, and abundance is already within you to make it happen. You have everything within you to make a major difference in your life and the lives of those around you. If you can see it within, you can manifest externally.

Law of Attraction says, "As within, so without." "As above, so below." Everything you want and desire is already at your disposal from within you. And this biblical principle is one that consistently escapes the mind of the religious who say they believe. Jesus said to His disciples, "you will receive power when the Holy Spirit comes on you" (Acts 1:8a, NIV). We have the power to manifest the supernatural. But, there are religious folk who still think that they cannot move the mountains that Jesus said they can move. Jesus said, "Because you have so little faith, truly, I tell you, if you have faith like a grain of mustard seed, you can say to this mountain, 'Move from here to there,' and it will move. Nothing will be impossible for you" (Matthew 17:20, NIV). That wasn't figurative. That was literal! But again, you have religious folk waiting to die to receive their pie in the sky instead of receiving it now. They would rather suffer now and then get what they think they deserve after they die. Does that make sense to you?

Understanding the presence and power of God within you is paramount to creating the dynamic life you can live in the present moment in the here and now. Asking God for big and miraculous things are small things to Him. God can create something out of nothing. He can turn your whole life completely around for the better. He can take you from abject poverty to miraculous prosperity. So, when you decide to create a life that you've never lived before, know that "nothing is impossible with God" (Luke 1:37, NIV), and that God will manifest that life so fast it will make your head spin.

From a Law of Attraction perspective, we are vibrational beings in a vibrational universe. It was Albert Einstein who stated, "whatever energy vibration you send out to the universe, you will attract into your life. That is why people are living the life they are living right now because of their vibration, or in other words, their thoughts, emotions, feelings, actions, and intention." If you can align these inner components of your inner world and your inner sight, you can create a mirroring external life. That is The Law of Attraction. Because when you change your internal vibrations, you will change your outer life. So, if the Divine presence of God is within co-creating your world based on your vibrations and imagination, Wow! Receiving what you want to be, what you want to do, and what you want to have is a foregone conclusion of aligned faith realized from a biblical perspective.

The Contradictions with Your Inner Vibration

Here's the reality of inner vibration within all of us. Our thoughts can contradict what we say we believe. We look at our current situation and we say, "There is no way I am going to manifest what I really want in life." "I am broke. I have bills to pay. There's no way I will ever really be financially rich." "Who am I kidding?" Bill collectors are calling. The mortgage or rent is due. Family members are depressed over their externally hopeless circumstances. And here you are trying to keep a positive attitude through it all. Yet, positive you must remain in order to rise above what seems to be an impossible scenario. But you must do it in order to align your energy, your inner sight, your vibration, your emotions, your thought, and your feelings to the level of what you want and for what you asked God for. It's imperative that you do. Without question, your inner man has to see happiness, love, success, prosperity, abundance within you through meditation, visualization, affirmation, journaling, and gratitude on a daily basis. You have to change the vibration of your inner world to match the vibration and frequency that you desire in our outer world. That's what faith looks like from a biblical and Law of Attraction perspective. Understand that your vibration attracts the same vibration. So if you're thinking negative thoughts and vibrating on what you don't have, you will attract a negative frequency creating negative results.

But I have bills! Join the human race. We all have bills. Stop focusing on the bills. Focus on your blessings. Focus on your home, your apartment, your car, your clothes, your beautiful family, your job. Focus on the good things that you have in life creating more good blessing flowing into your life.

Maintain the Positive Frequency Flowing from Within

By maintaining the positive frequency long enough, manifestation of that frequency will transmute into your reality. Because, what you think about most will eventually materialize in your life. If you think about negative things, you will attract negative things. But if you think about positive things of what you want and ask for, long enough, those things will manifest over time. That's not just a Universal Law, that's Scripture from a biblical perspective (Matthew 7:7-8).

Is what I'm talking about easy to manifest? Not always. And that's where resilience comes in. Resilience exists at the heart of what you really want out of life. When you do not walk in the direction of what you want, you die a slow death everyday with very little resistance in giving up on living.

Fear, doubt and uncertainty have to be the main emotional forces that keep people from pursuing their ideal goals and dreams. They fear the possibility of failure while at the same time hating the jobs that they feel they are forced to work. So when setbacks arise, without pursuing what they truly desire, they have very little energy to fight against anything they may not agree with. They merely settle to live a life that they do not like in the first place.

No Plan Is Perfect

But, with any plan, adjustments have to be incurred, setbacks will occur, but progress will be made if people are willing to stay faithful to the goals at hand. Because, when difficulties come knocking, you have to review what it is you truly want in your life. Again, Jesus told His disciples, *"Ask"* (Mark 11:24, NIV). Put another way, *"What do you want?"* Before you can accomplish the desire of your heart, you have to know what you exactly want. And with whatever you want, you have to know that you really want it. So, you need to clarify exactly what you want to accomplish in order to know where you want to go in life. If not, *you wander through life aimlessly tossed about like the waves of the sea (James 1:6, NIV)*. *"He that wavers is like a wave of the sea driven with the wind and tossed."* You have to be specific on what you want. James 1:8 reads, *"A double minded man is unstable in all his ways."* So, clarity is the key in asking for what you want. You have to know or figure out what you really want out of life in order to develop the resilience to withstand the negative waves that will occasionally try to destroy your goals and dreams.

You Have To Believe You Can Get What You Want

If you doubt and don't think you can get what you want, you might as well forget it. Jesus said, *"Whatever you ask for in prayer believe that you have received it, and it will be yours."* (Mark 11:24, NIV). Put another way, when we pray, we are to believe that we already have received what we want even before it has been manifested into our reality. He is talking about faith in what you want, believing that it is spiritually yours already, as you work your plan to make your answered prayer a concrete reality. He says, focus on your answered prayer from God through faith, knowing that it is in route into your reality through the actions you take to make what you want to materialize.

How Answered Prayer Works

God puts the people, the opportunities, and the resources in place for your answered prayer to become concrete reality. Only God can make something out of nothing. However, through our personal faith in the Almighty, believing that He can and will bring what we want and desire into our real world, our actions must reflect our belief in what God has already done in the spirit so that it is manifested in time and space in our tangible reality.

Out of Nothing to Something

There are thousands of rags to riches stories throughout the world from men and women who started with nothing but an idea. They were willing to risk failure in the pursuit of their dreams, because they had nothing to lose in the first place. People like Howard Schultz, the founder of Starbucks, Kenny Trout, the founder of Excel Communications, Oprah Winfrey, and Ralph Lauren all started with nothing but a dream that was eventually manifested into their own personal reality; and so can you.

From the Dream, Comes a Plan

Every success story starts with a dream that morphs into a plan that will be tweaked and adjusted again and again. They don't wait for everything to be perfect. They believe that with every setback there's a comeback. And when people tell them, it can't be done, they continue to resiliently move forward into an uncertain future. But they continue to choose to take chances that lead to their ultimate goals. Just know that every plan will be altered and sometimes completely changed. However, successful people experience troubles, just like you. Therefore, when the troubles come, and they will come, you continue to keep a positive attitude that inspires you to keep going no matter what. Quitting can never be an option in pursuing the life and career you desire to possess. Therefore, it is paramount that your plans must be galvanized in utter determination aligned with positive thoughts and a desired vision to manifest what you truly want.

With Your Plans Comes Determination to Manifest

If success is your only option in fulfilling your dreams, then your plans must be fueled by a determination that never quits, with the resiliency of determination. Someone once wrote, *"Some people succeed because they are destined, but most because they are determined"* – Unknown.

Jesus said, *"In this world, you will have tribulation, but be of good cheer, I have overcome the world" (John 16:33, KJV)*. We are all guaranteed to have trouble during the course of our lives, but with the right attitude, the good news is that we can overcome any adversity to achieve the goals we aspire to obtain, no matter what the disappointment or setback. With anything we face, we have the ability to bounce back from it, with the right attitude and with determination. But it all starts from within with the presence and power of God in helping you co-create.

From the Plan Comes the Action

At no point did any successful person expect their journey of success to be easy. In fact, most expected difficulties, detours, and roadblocks. Each person realized that an action plan had to be in place to succeed at what it was they were trying to accomplish. Their actions were a reflection of what they sought to manifest from within.

The good news of being resilient in your life is that with a strong belief in what you seek to manifest, it can come to fruition with a dream clarified by a plan worked through with the actions to move forward with the awesome help of someone greater than yourself, who I believe is Almighty God. Because with a strong faith in God and his unlimited power at your disposal, *"You can do all things through Him, who strengthens you" (Philippians 4:13, NASB)* as you resiliently press forward into a magnificent future. Just don't give up on what you want in living a full abundant life. With that in mind, it's time to align your thoughts with your vibrational frequency to manifest the impossible. You can do it!

Call to Action

1. Align your thoughts with your vibration.
2. Vibration attracts to the same vibration.
3. Your thoughts can contradict what you say you believe.

4. The Kingdom of God within co-creates with your thoughts, emotions, feelings, actions, and overall vibration.
5. Block negative thoughts while focusing on positive ones.
6. Resiliently maintain your positive frequency long enough to manifest to transmute your new outer reality.

Chapter 8

From a Biblical Perspective – Take Action!

> *See a man diligent and skillful in his business? He will stand before kings. He shall not stand before obscure men (Proverbs 22:29, TAB)*

So, the pieces of the puzzle to the Law of Attraction from a biblical perspective is to take action by creating a daily morning routine of gratitude.

1. "Give thanks to the Lord, for He is good. His love endures forever. Give thanks to the God of gods" (107:1,2, NIV). Give thanks daily for what you have in the present moment; the roof over your head, your transportation, your partner, your children, your parents, your job, your health, your abundance, and on and on. Every morning and every night, "Give thanks to the Lord." This takes diligence, even when you don't feel like it. Gratitude is a daily commitment that pays multiple dividends.

2. "When you pray, go into your room, close the door and pray to your Father, who is unseen. Then your Father, who sees what is done in secret, will reward you" (Matthew 6:6, NIV). Law of Attraction says, ask, believe that it is already yours. Feel it with unwavering faith, feeling good about it, feeling happy about it, and then receive it in God's time as He ultimately manifests it. It's on the way.

3. Be sure to visualize what you want to materialize while visualizing the end result, with feeling. Feel that you already have what you want now. Inner happiness is the fuel to manifest your dreams. Write your visions in your journal. "And the Lord answered me: Write the vision; make it plain on table, so he may run who reads it" (Habakkuk 2:2 ESV).

4. Don't worry about HOW you'll get what you want. The presence and power of God in you, as His temple, with your subconscious in conjunction to the universe will manifest the HOW. It's on the way in His time.

5. Be sure to diligently decide what you want, believe that you have it, believe that you deserve it, and believe that it's for you in the present moment.

6. Believe in yourself knowing that you are "fearfully and wonderfully made" (Psalm 139:14, NIV). Because if you don't believe in yourself, limiting beliefs about what you desire, will block the blessings God had in store for you.

7. So, Be Intentional about what you want, with elevated feelings of joy and expectation leading to prosperity and abundance. "Be strong in the Lord and in the power of His might" (Ephesians 6:10, NKJV). Say to yourself, "I will prevail." "I will succeed." "I am 'more than a conqueror through Him who loves' me" (Romans 8:37, NIV). And say it like you mean it, with feeling!

Do these seven things in your pray room daily along with meditation to clear your mind of negative thoughts, stress, and disbelief. "For still the vision awaits it's appointed time; it hastens to the end – it will not lie. If it seems slows, wait for it; it will surely come; it will not delay" (Habakkuk 2:2-3, ESV).

While you're meditating and praying in your prayer closet, try listening to some Theta Music. You can find some on YouTube for free. Listen to it to open up all the energy centers in your mind, body, and soul consciously tapping into your subconscious mine with feelings of love, joy, happiness, and peace.

Once you've spent time in prayer, meditation, visualization, continue to transform your mind with powerful positive affirmations regarding family, love, money, prosperity, abundance and wealth.

1. I feel Rich
2. I see abundance everywhere
3. I deserve to live abundantly
4. I am a money magnet
5. I am loved
6. I love me
7. I am blessed
8. I have the power to attract wealth
9. I have the power to attract love
10. I am happy
11. I am wealthy right now
12. My self-worth is increasing
13. I am confident always

"So do not fear, for I am with you; do not be dismayed, for I am your God. I will strengthen you and help you; I will uphold you with my righteous right hand" (Isaiah 41:10, NIV).

Look yourself in the mirror and say, "You are awesome!" "You are going to accomplish great things!" "Keep it up!" "You are headed in the right direction!"

It's More Than Just Saying, "All You Need Is Jesus."

For the religious folk out there, when people come to you with real life problems and struggles, they need more than just "All you need is Jesus." They need a genuine understanding of Faith that works. When they come asking for prayer regarding financial struggles. Give them a plan of action that works. They have been focusing their attention on their brokenness and their lack. They have been wallowing in what they don't want instead of what they do want. So, religious folk tell them, "I want you to go out and buy a composite journal, and I want you to start writing everyday what your perfect day looks like." "I want you to thank God everyday for all the good things in your life now." "Then, I want you to start writing down your goals that you want to accomplish and thank God in advance for the answered prayers that you asked for, in advance." Say, "Thank you Lord for all the money flowing into my bank account now." "Thank you for the prosperity flowing in my life daily." And since many of these individuals are stressed, tell them to take 3 to 5 minutes alone by themselves every morning to just take 5 to 10 deep cleansing breaths while focus on nothing but that present moment. Tell them to make it a habit, praising God every day for the miracles now flowing into their lives. Give them some affirmations starting with "I am" to say each morning, at lunch, during the day, and at night before bed: "I am blessed." "I am wealthy." "I am attracting money into my life." "I do appreciate my partner." These are daily affirmations that people struggling with real issues need to speak to themselves, and what better place to receive these powerful instructions but from their religious leaders and friends. Because they need more than just a Bible verse and pretty prayers. They need real instructional tools that they can apply every day to get them to the abundant level above where they currently are.

If you attract what you think, people need to change the way they think to change their current life situation. So, people who are struggling in various ways need to receive instructions like The Law of Attraction from a biblical perspective. These empowering principles will change a multitude of peoples live for the better if we can just open our minds for the purpose of helping struggling people change their lives in a very positive way.

Know that life is meant to be abundant. We were meant to be creators of our own lives through the presence and power of God who resides within our earthly temples. Thinking takes diligent action knowing that we become what we think about. That's The Law of Attraction as we are told to "Let this mind be in you which was also in Christ Jesus" (Philippians 2:5, KJV). So, let us focus on what we want, and not what we don't want knowing that through the power of God in us and around us, we will create and manifest a Law of Attraction life based on biblical principles.

"Now unto Him that is able to keep you from falling, and to present you faultless before the presence of His glory with exceeding joy, to the only wise God our Savior, be glory and majesty, dominion and power, both now and ever. Amen" (Jude 1:24-25). Now that you've read it, it's time to take diligent action to manifest it from a biblical perspective utilizing the power of the inner eye with the power and presence of God and the Universal at your disposal.

"Ask," then follow The Law of Attraction from the Reap/Sow Principles of Faith, then watch the power of your imagination manifest into your external reality.

In A Brief Summary

1. Decide what you want (Intention).
2. Believe that you got what you want (Faith).
3. See yourself with what you want (Visualize it).

4. Feel yourself experiencing what you want (Elevated motions).
5. The power of God is around you and within you (One with God).
6. Jesus said, "Very truly I tell you, whoever believes in me will do the works I have been doing, and they will do even greater things than these, because I am going to the Father. And I will do whatever you ask in my name, so that the Father may be glorified in the Son. You may ask me for anything in my name, and I will do it" (John 14:12-14, NIV). Repeat after me, "Ask" and it will be manifested.
7. Transform your mind to believe in yourself, your own abilities, your own thought, and your own intuition, being one with God and his creative powers. Be transformed with a renewed mindset. From there, get excited about what is happen in your life. Allow these Law of Attraction principles from a biblical perspective manifest in your new reality. Practice it daily allowing the blessings to flow as you give gratitude to the Most High God on a daily basis visualizing the life you truly desire to manifest. You have the power!

www.ingramcontent.com/pod-product-compliance
Lightning Source LLC
Chambersburg PA
CBHW071508070526
44578CB00001B/474